Life's

L**ophole**

Awareness

For The Human Mind

SOMETHING YOU NEED TO FIND

Michael Joseph Smith

For Stacey & Dylan, with love

Email: contact@growbyreading.com

Website: growbyreading.com

ISBN: 979-8-9902706-3-3

To my oldest brother, who never had a fair chance—and to all those listening—may the wisdom herein help guide you toward your desired path—an opportunity my brother never had.

Preface

I originally wrote this book for myself—to distill valuable principles for ease of reference. But these insights will benefit you as well. This concise guide presents fundamental principles to boost self-awareness and cultivate a positive mindset for the best possible outcomes in life.

While some ideas are undervalued or simply overlooked, I encourage you to take the time and explore this book with an open mind and draw a conclusion that serves you best! This book isn't about me—it's about you and the power that resides within your own conscious mind to shape your health, happiness, and your entire life!

These principles are interconnected, designed to serve your growth and well-being. You may already be familiar with some, if not all of them, but reviewing what you know deepens its impact. With its straightforward design, this book is meant to be revisited whenever needed, helping you to fully integrate the wisdom you value— which was my reasoning for writing this book for my own purposeful use!

Note: This book is not a substitute for professional medical advice, diagnosis, or treatment. Always consult with a qualified healthcare provider regarding your physical or mental health whenever a concern exist. Positive thinking and mindfulness alone cannot cure medical conditions, nor can the body heal itself from every ailment. By offering additional support in the pursuit of your most aware, healthiest, happiest self, this book is intended to complement, not replace, traditional medicine. By reading this book, you acknowledge that the author assumes no responsibility or liability for any actions taken based on its content.

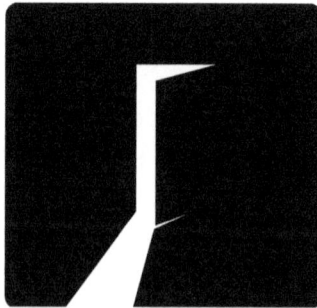

Fed up with any part of life? You're not alone—you're in the right place and in good hands. Today, you can start to take a stand—for you!

Intro

By definition, a loophole is a hidden advantage—a way to achieve what seems impossible. Life's loophole is **Awareness** in the conscious mind.

Awareness is the most powerful force of the human mind. It means knowing what's happening, why it's happening, and what you can do about it. *Without awareness, you're like a ship with no direction—just drifting…*

Awareness exists only in your conscious mind, working alongside the memory and the preprogrammed unconscious mind. Awareness is the key to connecting with your desires, accessing inner wisdom, and taking responsibility for your actions. Without it, you're merely reacting to life instead of consciously shaping it!

Your conscious mind powers self-awareness, discipline, motivation, growth, compassion, and purpose. The more you exercise awareness, the more control you have over your life. *In time, you'll come to recognize that awareness in the conscious mind is the most powerful action you'll ever find!*

Think about these facts: Life is a collection of memories—some uplifting, others painful. These experiences shape your health, mindset, and reality. And what you continually project—positive or negative—always returns back to you. Being aware of these universal truths is crucial, and how you use them will define your life, as it always has and always will—whether consciously or not! *So, roamin' around clueless is not an option anymore!*

No Matter what area of life you desire to improve or what you intend to accomplish, the formula to success goes unchanged—such a formula is outlined here and the journey toward a more desirable reality can begin today!

With focus, intention, accountability, awareness, and persistence you can transform your health, reduce pain, find your soulmate, excel in your career, and reshape your reality to match your true desires!

What This Book Is About:

- **The Human Brain's Three Main Parts:** The Conscious Mind, Memory, and the Unconscious Mind—how they work together to influence your health and life.

- **How Memories & Beliefs Can Harm You:** Negative beliefs and unresolved memories can damage your health, manifesting as pain, aging, and even illness.

- **The Power of Thought:** Your mindset attracts corresponding experiences—what you focus on, you bring on—*which may not be serving you well!*

- **Accountability & Growth:** Personal accountability and practical routines bring you closer to your potential and dreams!

How This Book Is Structured:

- **Principles for Health & Fulfillment:** Foundational concepts to *revisit as needed.*

- **Wisdom Review:** Key points for reflection—*every other month or so.*

- **Practice Section:** Steps for emotional, physical, and intellectual excellence—*revisit daily and adjust as needed.*

Some limitations are beyond your control, but you can always strive to become your best self. ***Although limitations do exist, you don't know what they are until they're met!***

This book exists to help all readers achieve a more informed, healthier, happier, and fulfilling life! *Life is short, and no one's life is more valuable than another's!* If that thought bothers you, then you might not be ready. ***But*** if you're brave enough and ready for more, please proceed forward!

Note: This book is not intended to conflict with any religious beliefs, nor does it establish a religion of its own. Instead, it offers universal truths and principles available to everyone, designed only to complement any core values you may already hold within.

Take a moment to find and cut out your bookmarks located on the very last page of this book. But no peeking ahead—you'll get there soon enough! Use these bookmarks to hold your place and help highlight the parts that inspire you most!

The guiding light is within you. The map to access it is as follows...

Principles for Health and Fulfillment

In This Section:

- **The Mind & Body Connection**
  The link between thoughts, emotions, and physical health.

- **The Law of Attraction**
  The power of intention and mindset used for shaping your reality.

- **Accountability**
  Taking ownership of your choices and actions for a more empowered life.

- **Lifestyle Philosophy**
  Defining personal values and daily habits that align with a fulfilling life.

These principles serve as the foundation for cultivating a balanced, mindful, and purposeful way of living. By integrating them into your life, you can unlock a deeper sense of well-being and fulfillment.

We start with the *Mind & Body Connection* theory first, because, *without good physical health and energy, it's hard to accomplish anything!*

Once you turn the page, your wisdom will take root and blossom fruit—and there'll be no goin' back—only forward... more consciously!

The Mind & Body Connection

The *Mind & Body Connection* theory is rooted in the influence of the uncontrollable part of your brain, specifically, the preprogrammed, perfectly intelligent, always right mind. From now on, we'll refer to this area of the brain as the *background mind*.

A universal intelligence energy field serves all living beings through their *background mind*. This field provides the perfect intelligence specific to each organism—from humans to honeybees—ensuring their basic functionality for life and survival, specific to the being the universe is serving. This intelligence allows us the ability to live and continue doing so without conscious thought.

The universal intelligence energy field is also present to serve back to us what we emit (thoughts and feelings), just as prescribed by the *Law of Attraction*.

The background mind (Perfect Intelligent Mind) is unchanged and always correct for the life-being it's ingrained in. Your background mind gains perfect intelligence at the onset of fetal formation and is said to be the very first evidence of life creation.

The background mind is the area of the brain that governs all bodily functionality with the top priority of survival, at all costs, even to the point of total physiological exhaustion. When immediate threats to life are absent, or not presently sensed or signaled, the focus shifts from survival to: protection, repair, and renewal—ensuring readiness for future challenges and further survival.

The background mind is aware of everything happening within and around the body and has the ability to control all bodily organs to achieve its primary goal of survival. This becomes concerning in cases of constant stress, whether physical or emotional, as the mind and therefore the body must prioritize immediate survival (handling of stress) over long-term well-being. As a result, internal healing and protective processes are halted, all due to constant stress. Therefore, always aim to keep any form of stress *short-term*—to include eating, drinking, exercising, or being emotionally upset.

The act of surviving and handling stress is exhaustive—not only to the mind but also to the body. A relived traumatic life experience or continual bad lifestyle habits are extremely stressful on the mind and body—and as with anything else in continuation, continual stress is extremely tiring and thus very ill-serving!

The mind and body are interconnected via the background mind, which, again, is the perfect intelligent, preprogrammed portion of your brain. The background mind is in direct control of your physiological functionalities and is never directly controlled *but is influenced* by the signals it receives from your *conscious mind* (sensory data, feelings, and desired movement) and your *memory bank mind* (beliefs and emotions). The background mind takes orders from both the conscious mind and the memory bank portion of the brain, resulting in an appropriate, always right physiological response in accordance with the signaling the background mind is receiving. *Note: This medical truth may not be serving you well!* Let's explore this process further—keeping it general for our purposes:

The Conscious Mind

The conscious mind interprets sensory data, such as sight, sound, and touch, and sends signals to the memory bank for a reference against a belief for the data sensed. The resultant data signals from the memory go to the background mind for appropriate physiological actions, resulting in outward and/or inward reactions. The conscious mind may also send a signal to the memory bank for reference against a more simple action, like moving your arm. The conscious mind is the center of awareness and decision-making. It relies on the memory portion of the brain for learned knowledge (beliefs) and physical abilities, avoiding the need to relearn everything, over-and-over again.

The Memory Bank

This part of your mind stores beliefs and emotions tied to memories, shaping how your background mind responds when a memory or belief is thought of. When negative memories dominate, reliving them repeatedly triggers stress, leading to inner exhaustion and potentially physical symptoms like lower back or neck pain. In contrast, recalling happy memories has the opposite effect, fostering positive emotions that support your well-being.

The Background Mind

This is your body's survival engine. Its highest priority is survival—responding to perceived threats, whether real or imagined (replayed negative memories or bogus self-harming beliefs), to keep you alive. It controls bodily functions meant to protect, repair, and rebuild, but it can also divert resources from these processes when under stress because stress, no matter the form, is viewed as a threat to survival, at least initially! If stress is prolonged, the resultant scenario can cause ill health and even physical pain as a result of physiological exhaustion. The background mind can also divert oxygen from an area of the body to induce physical pain as a diversion technique meant to shield the conscious mind from emotional distress (another act of survival)—where recognizing such emotional pain is more harmful than focusing on harmless, psychologically induced physical pain—*or at least that's what the uncontrollable, preprogrammed, background mind thinks is best!*

Stress and Its Impact

Stress disrupts the background mind's ability to perform its essential functionalities, such as ordering the immune system to protect and the recuperative system to heal and rebuild. Stress can be categorized into two types, *short-term* and *long-term*:

- **Short-Term Stress:** Typically manageable and often beneficial in moderation, such as drinking, eating, and exercising.
- **Long-Term Stress:** Prolonged exposure to negativity or false–positive threats that lead to illness, chronic pain, and chronic fatigue. Examples: suppressed emotions, negative self-beliefs, replayed negative memories, and harmful external factors like poor diet, lack of rest, poor activity level, and even poor air quality.

So again, the background mind prioritizes survival during stress, halting protective and reparative functionalities performed by the body, internally. Over time, this leads to physical and emotional exhaustion, resulting in unexplainable physical pain and even illness or disease due to the inability to protect against invaders and heal against breakdown at your body's otherwise more capable level. To optimize your physiological system, minimize stress and support the mind and body through practices of self-awareness, *Baggage Claiming* (discussed later), meditation, diet, exercise, and quality sleep.

Key Intellectual Concepts That Fill Your Mind

Your background mind knows about everything going on—in and around your body.

When it comes to negative emotions and feelings—defuse what you can't lose (negative memories) and express what's being suppressed (intense inner negativity).

Emotional stress comes in many forms: memories, bogus beliefs about oneself, and repressed intense feelings.

Your thoughts reflect your currently conscious beliefs and feelings as well as what you're generally focused on—*which may not be serving you well!*

Note: Thoughts, feelings, and beliefs can be harmful (negative) or helpful (positive). It's up to you to exercise awareness and perception to notice the difference. You need to be accountable and practice appropriately for your own well-being.

Your emotions reflect your memories when thought of, whether by the intense nature of a memory itself or as a reminder of a memory due to a similar, current life event or your life reality in general.

So again, a memory can be replayed (relived) due to its impact on your conscious mind or by the repetitive nature of your reality—your life.

A memory can never be erased, nor can you rid yourself of its associated emotions, however, their impact on you can be reduced—we'll learn more about that soon.

A memory can be perceived as either negative or positive, and a memory's associated emotions reflect the same.

Your inner intensities accumulate from memories, beliefs, stressors, or all of the above and become harmful when not consciously confronted (aware of) and properly dealt with (expressed). Awareness, accountability, updating bogus negative beliefs, and practicing a positive, hopeful, and active lifestyle will help slow down and even dissolve such a buildup. *Consult with a professional therapist to help further your progress, where necessary.*

Intense Suppressed Emotions

Common types of repressed, negative internal pressures include: frustration, anger, rage, abandonment, resentment, grief, low self-worth, poor self-image, anxiousness, and shame—feelings that constantly trouble you and only serve you negatively. These types of feelings also reflect as your personality traits and mannerisms—all of which can be eased and improved on *with awareness and desire.*

Recognizing and dealing with negative internal intensity is the most important concept of the *Mind & Body Connection* theory. To fully understand and address your inner emotional pain, you must identify the reasons for its formation and the factors contributing to its continuation. Intense negativity can begin at childhood, accumulate over time, and persist throughout our entire life—affecting our: health, happiness, physical pain level, and overall success.

Note: We don't suppress positive feelings like happiness, because it's more enjoyable to share such with the world. We're never ashamed or embarrassed of our positive emotions. Even though we have to calm our excitement at times, we never repress positive feelings—only negative ones.

Defuse What You Can't Lose and Lessen What's Suppressed with Healthy Expressions

So how do you defuse a negative emotion, whether attached to a perceived negative memory or as a result of accumulated daily life events? *With your aware, conscious mind*—recognize a negative memory that's replaying or the intensely suppressed emotion that's determining your mood, then exercise your *Baggage Claiming* technique (up next) to defuse or dissolve your inner negativity.

The Baggage Claim Technique (placed again in the *Practice Section* for ease of reference)

- **Have awareness of what's bothering you:** What and why it is, and who's involved.

- **Have gratitude** for coming to this point of recognition. *It's hard work making time for self-care and self-reflection, especially when it comes to taking account of your baggage.* ← *You're not alone here — WE ALL HAVE BAGGAGE!*

- **Be thankful for getting past** the negative memory or stressors causing you continual negativity. *If you're not in the clear, then make a conscious change to make it so!*

- **Have awareness and exercise perspective:** Why it's negative, why it's so impactful, and how you can make it better — for you!

- **Exercise reason:** Is it really worth all it's doing to you (internal stress) and all it's taking from you (health and happiness)?

- **Have accountability for your involvement** in the event and your ability to move forward more positively from it!

- **Find the smallest bit of growth.** A lesson learned from an event and gratitude expressed for the lesson learned will only serve you positively — helping you move on from the negativity!

- **Forgive all those involved, including yourself**, and let them forgive you as well! *To forgive doesn't mean to accept or allow, it just means to think less intensely negative. So, forgive for your own sake — no one else's.*

- **Shift focus** from the ill-serving memory or inner intensities and *think about your loved ones and the dream life you're about to embark on!*

- **Be proud and empowered** by the strength you have exercised to confront your inner negativity to reduce its negative effects.

- **Go express yourself in a healthy fashion** to further release your inner negativity via a positive, expressive activity like: dancing, singing, jogging, boxing, or even painting!

Empowering you to confront your past and transform your inner negativity for your own direct benefit — while shifting your focus toward positivity — is the ultimate goal of this book for all its readers!

Bogus Beliefs Can Cause Internal Stress & Hinder Success

Beliefs hold power, but not all are true or helpful. Some beliefs, like feeling unworthy, incapable, unloved, or undesirable, can be deeply damaging. Recognize these beliefs as being bogus and update them as they have never served you well nor ever will!

Beliefs are not fixed—they are changeable and updatable with strong conviction. Just as beliefs were formed through repeated thoughts and emotions, so too can they be updated. Start by consciously creating a new belief, pairing it with positive emotions and reinforcing it constantly through practice and focus until it becomes your new truth. *Always believe and feel good about all you know—your beliefs!*

Growth requires letting go of outdated beliefs. For example, as a child, you may have believed monsters were hiding under the bed or in the closet. But with growth and reason, you realized there where no monsters in your room and as a result, your beliefs changed. **Beliefs change when awareness and reasoning grow!** Similarly, beliefs about yourself—like being limited, incapable, or unwanted—can also be updated. Focus on a new belief, celebrate its validity, know with confidence that it's true, and continue to *kick-butt* making it so!

Your beliefs shape your reality, so choose them wisely. Believe in your greatness, embrace your potential, and let your life reflect the powerful truth of who you are becoming! Practice a lifestyle that supports and doesn't contradict your beliefs— your valued truth!

Diversion From Emotional Pain

When the background mind detects unresolved negative emotions, it may redirect the conscious mind's focus to physical pain as a survival tactic. This prevents emotional distress from overwhelming your conscious mind, where the presence of ongoing distress is overdue for resolution and is likely only going to further deteriorate your mental well-being. Examples of *psychologically induced physical pain* include chronic neck and/or lower back pain, often labeled as "unexplainable" by traditional medicine. A cover-up approach is typically applied to unexplainable pain, managed with medications, physical therapy, and even surgery—all efforts to resolve the pain but not the root cause itself—because it's unknown (emotional). Such practices only lead to pain continuation, likely in a new area of the background mind's choosing. *So, treat the cause, not just the symptoms, with Baggage Claiming!*

Combat Psychologically Induced Pain:

- **Awareness:** Recognize unexplainable pain as a potential sign of repressed emotions or physical exhaustion due to continual internal stress, whether by lifestyle habits and/or inner negativity (mindset).

- **Confrontation:** Actively identify and address suppressed or negative emotions. Use mindfulness, your *Baggage Claiming* technique, therapy, self-reflection, and healthy expressive activities to release negative energy.

- **Affirmation:** Speak to your pain. Acknowledge it as harmless and focus on the underlying emotional causes instead of the physical sensation itself. Many times, this eases physical pain due to your conscious awareness of the diversion tactic of the background mind and your conscious desire to make it better.

Whenever you're faced with unexplainable pain—even pain you assume is part of normal aging—think again. Ask yourself: *Is there something deep down bothering me?* Confront your baggage for what and why it is, and concern yourself with how to consciously and positively deal with it. Sometimes, awareness, confrontation, and problem-solving with the right questions can work wonders. The common conclusion that pain or breakdown is just "the normal aging process" is crap—your body is likely more capable and more willing to stay younger for longer than you ever thought possible! *Your mind and body want to live and thrive as long as possible*—you just have to gain awareness of this and support their quest for it!

Aging Gracefully

Yesterday's experiences shape today's health. Perceived negative memories influence negative emotions, negative beliefs, and an overall undesirable state of being—making awareness and *Bagging Claiming* necessary for *"aging gracefully!"*

The Body—A Self-Healing Full Maintenance Facility

Your body is designed to heal, regulate itself, and deal with stress while prioritizing survival first. The physical toll of this ongoing process often manifests itself as "aging" but it's primarily due to physiological exhaustion from continual excess stress and/or a lack of healthy lifestyle practices, such as quality rest. By reducing stress and negativity and supporting your body's natural abilities, you can slow the aging process, including disease formation. By supporting your body's ability to heal and renew, you promote vitality and longevity. To a degree, you can even reverse accelerated aging associated with the environment you've likely been exposing yourself to!

Note: When you prepare properly and achieve quality sleep, your mind and body can heal and protect at their highest capacity. So remember: Time taken away from quality rest—is time taken away from your personal best!

*A memory can be just as stressful when remembered as it was when first created. Your surroundings—or even your general mindset—can reignite negative emotions, ultimately affecting your mood and your complete well-being. **This is relevant to every human being, so awareness of this is a must!***

The Bigger Picture

The *Mind & Body Connection* theory is a powerful framework for understanding and improving your health, happiness, and the reality you see unfold in front of you. By minimizing stress, promoting quality rest, addressing suppressed emotions, and fostering positive beliefs and thinking, you empower your body to not only survive but to heal, protect, rebuild, and thrive! Remember: *Positive within, positive out, for a positive internal result and a positive rebound!*

Note: Seek therapy to address intense suppressed emotions or traumatic memories. Professional guidance can help defuse negativity and ease or prevent physical pain caused by emotional avoidance. Therapy can enable constructive conversations for reflection and pressure relief, helping you to better handle past and future stressors —even to the point of avoiding further accumulation of such baggage!

Unlike other beings, humans possess the unique ability to consciously think, reason, and focus, granting us the power to greatly influence our own realities. The question is: *How will you harness this power?* With conscious continual awareness—that's how! Up next, the *Law of Attraction* theory will help propel your success even further!

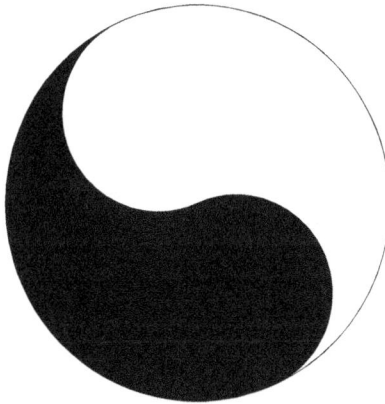

Peace in the mind brings strength to the frame—both play a part in life's game.

The Law of Attraction: The Power of Thought

The *Law of Attraction* is simple: Everything in the universe is connected by a universal energy field—the same field that serves your perfectly intelligent mind also rebounds the energy of your conscious thinking back to you in kind. For the purposes of the *Law of Attraction* theory, the energy we emit shapes the reality we experience. The frequencies of our thoughts and emotions create scientifically measurable vibrations that the universe mirrors back to us as our life circumstances —our ever-developing reality.

To benefit from this universal law, focus on positivity, because what you constantly concentrate on, whether good or bad, becomes your reality. Your thoughts shape your life, so it's vital to be consciously aware of your mindset. If you expect bad luck, you're likely to attract it. However, by focusing on gratitude, hope, and joy, you invite better outcomes into your life! The *Emissions Check* technique, described in the *Practice Section* of this book, provides a routine for checking in and course-correcting your mindset when necessary. *The goal is simple: Positive Surround, Positive Within, Positive Out, for a Positive Rebound!* Easy enough, right? It may vary from day to day; however, with increased awareness, consistent practice, and positive intention, you can achieve greatly—just as you dream (focus on)!

Visualization is a powerful tool. When you vividly imagine your goals with strong positive emotions, your mind starts to perceive these visions as achievable realities —even to the point of perceiving such visions as real memories from your past. This process isn't just daydreaming—it's creating a mental blueprint that helps align your energy with your desires. The principle is simple: Take a moment on a daily basis, as a routine, and visualize your dream until it becomes second nature in your mind. Gratitude amplifies this process, so feel thankful for what you visualize as if it's already part of your life—because, in a sense, it is, because you're focusing on it and you're feeling what it's like to live it! *So think it, 'til you make it, come true for you!*

Try to radiate positivity with every part of your being. Here's a key point to help reinforce the idea: *Want it—don't need it.* Desperation generates negative energy, which blocks your progress. Whether it's positive or negative, you get what you constantly emit, and being desperate or disappointed as a result of waiting, results in a negative mindset. So, respect and trust the process, and note that the journey is just as important as the goal itself. Life—*the universal energy field*—will deliver what you need in its own way and on its own time-frame. *So focus on enjoying the ride instead of rushing to the finish line!*

Remember: Energy flows where attention goes—always!

Focus on abundance, not lack. Give to receive for pure, positive reasons, separate from what you want in return. Be generous with positivity, kindness, and respect—such will be returned to you all the same!

Be thankful for who you currently are and all you currently have because that's a positive mindset. Be hopeful and excited about all you can improve on and achieve because that's positive motivation to positively receive!

In summary, believe in your dreams, act with gratitude, and trust in your ever-unfolding journey. Success builds confidence, and each win strengthens your ability to aim higher! With focus, patience, and positivity, the possibilities are truly extraordinary—just like the potential of your aware, conscious mind!

Your mind's a magnet, strong and direct—it attracts what you think and the energy you project.

Accountability: Transform Your Life, Responsibility

Accountability is about owning your reality with self-awareness, honesty, and a willingness to focus on yourself to grow for your own sake. It's the ability to look inward and ask, *What can I do to improve this situation?* Instead of pointing fingers or blaming external factors, accountability shifts the focus to what you *can* control—which is your attitude, your actions, and your aware, conscious mindset!

Where we lack accountability, we seek something else to change or improve. In reality, although we don't even have full control over our own circumstances, *we do however, have full control of our attitude and our conscious thinking!* So, whenever you're faced with an undesirable situation or result—or even life in general—look at yourself, be honest, and ask yourself:

- *What could I have done for a better result?*
- *What can I do now to make it better?*
- *What can I learn from this and improve on for a better outcome, from now on?*

Not only is such an approach positive, it also carries with it the intent to solve a problem. In a sense, it's motivation to improve—to make a change—it's self-respect in motion! With such a thought process, not only are you more capable of solving problems, but also, while thinking more positively, you're less stressed! All the above are the foundational goals of this book—*less long-term stress, greater self-regard, and more positivity expressed!*

Accountability isn't about blaming anyone or anything—not even yourself. It's about learning and improving. When you take responsibility for your actions and your role in your life's events, you transform obstacles into stepping stones toward a higher existence!

By practicing accountability, you empower yourself to face challenges with a problem-solving and positive attitude—*the most capable approach of all!* Life isn't about what happens *to* you, but what happens *for* you. Every experience, even the difficult ones, carries with it a lesson to be learned. Lessons may be painful at times, but there's always wisdom to be gained nonetheless. When you embrace this mindset, you unlock personal growth, build confidence, and pave the way for more satisfying outcomes. *There's not much in life we can truly control. Our aware, conscious mindset is likely the only thing we truly own!*

It goes without saying that some life events truly suck. Some are so unimaginable and can take your breath away. Those types of experiences are hard to process and even harder to move past. But once something happens—and we all go through things we'd rather not have happen—there's nothing we can do to reverse time or get it back. It's just gone—and what's done is done. So, make the most of an event, even when there's nothing to make of it, and move on from it the best you can. *Because, everyone who's ever loved you only wants you to live happily again—no matter how bad the life event.*

Key Principles of Accountability:

- **Ask the Right Questions:** Use "what" and "how" questions that focus on yourself, and not others: *What could I have done differently? How can I improve?*
- **Control What You Can:** You can't control others, but you can control your reactions, choices, mindset, and motivation to move forward positively.
- **Shift Negativity:** Turn setbacks into opportunities for growth. Defuse negative emotions, such as those associated with failure, with a problem-solving approach. Find satisfaction in your efforts to learn and grow, and in your determination to move beyond challenges.
- **Foster Understanding:** When others disappoint or upset you, consider what they may be dealing with in their personal lives that you can't see. Respond with patience, compassion, and positive intentions instead of building anger and resentment.

Note: You can't please others and you can't change others—so don't even try. Don't allow the actions of others to determine your own happiness. Don't allow the actions of others to build rage or resentment inside you. Either way, be accountable for you —inward and outwardly, today and forever!

The Benefits of Accountability:

- **Personal Growth:** Wisdom gained from your experiences—instead of frustration gained from excuse making!
- **Confidence:** Empowered knowing you can influence your future—but it's only up to you.
- **Acceptance:** Inner peace by acknowledging what is and focusing on what you can change.
- **Satisfaction & Heightened Self-Regard:** Gained from your proactive approach to life and through your intentions to make a change, because your actions prove you're worthy of it!

We learn lessons in life by finding at least the smallest bit of growth from an event— and only you can learn your lessons.

By viewing and experiencing life as a series of lessons to be learned, you come to understand that *you can't really fail at anything*. Life is a journey of lessons, and understanding this fact can help motivate you to upgrade your feelings about yourself, your life experiences, and the whole world around you!

Approach each lesson in life with gratitude and curiosity and you'll discover that even red lights can lead to green-light moments—*or at least provide you the time to reflect on whether your current path truly leads to your desired landing!*

The principles of *Accountability* directly support the principles of the *Law of Attraction* and the principles for optimal health of the mind and body, as prescribed by the *Mind & Body Connection* theory.

Again: *Positively Surround → Positive Within → Positive Out → For a Positive Rebound!*

Next, we'll wrap up this area of the book with a *Lifestyle Philosophy* that supports the *Law of Attraction* and the *Mind & Body Connection* theory while highlighting *Accountability* for embodying all of the above!

Face to face, no place to flee—what can I do? It's all on me.

Your Lifestyle Philosophy

A lifestyle philosophy is your way of life, reflecting your demeanor, confidence level, attractiveness, intentions, energy, and your level of determination. Those individuals who seem to have it all figured out aren't lucky—they live with intention. Their positive energy, confidence level, and focus create an aura that attracts success. And while some of us aren't naturally wired this way, we can adopt a similar mindset and an *Accountable Lifestyle* to align with the *Law of Attraction* and the *Mind & Body Connection* theory—done so with our aware, influential, conscious mind!

A positive *Lifestyle Philosophy* is about cherishing today and being excited for tomorrow. It's about loving life and sharing it with others. It's about finding joy, even in challenging times, where little is likely to be found. It's a mindset of saying, "If I gotta ride a bull (this life), then I'm gonna ride the heck out of it and enjoy every moment of it!"

The Foundation of a Positive Philosophy

Adopt a mindset that focuses on confidence, joy, and optimism. Visualize what you want and trust that it's already forming in your life—live it as if it's already real. Approach challenges as opportunities to learn, grow, and to prove your toughness– your resilience. When setbacks occur, extract a lesson, express gratitude for the lesson learned, and move forward with a strong sense of purpose. And when learning lessons, don't repeat yourself. Try not to learn the same lesson twice—*'cause learnin' the same lesson twice don't make it twice as right!*

Recognize Your Inner Genius

Your Inner Genius is used to align your lifestyle with your intentions—your dreams. Everyone has an Inner Genius—a wellspring of wisdom that grows with every lesson learned and every life event experienced. You have an Inner Genius—your unique ability to solve problems, gain perspective, and navigate life. Trust it. Pause, reflect, and listen to it. It's time to trust in yourself—your intuition, your *Inner Genius!* No matter what others have said or how you may have doubted yourself in the past, your Inner Genius is ready to guide you—*all you gotta do is ask, listen, and act accordingly!*

So What, Now What?

Adopt a "So what? Now, what do I need to do?" mentality when stuff gets nuts! Life may not always go your way, but every experience teaches a valuable lesson. Embrace those lessons and let them propel you forward with fluidity. *Just like the flow of water in the ocean—move with ease, adapt effortlessly to your surroundings while maintaining your depth and power.*

Transforming Negativity into Growth

Life isn't without hardship, but your reactions make all the difference. Trauma and adversity don't have to define you.

Think: *There aren't many bad days—only bad moments to learn from and move the heck on from!*

Remember: *You can't erase a memory, but you can reduce its negative hold on your health and happiness! With conscious effort and positive thinking, you can defuse and release negativity and reclaim your happiness! You can, just as you always have, shape your future life—'cept this time, you're gonna do it as you see it vividly in your aware, positive, in-control, conscious mind!*

Character Traits to Live By

Be self-aware, accountable, honest, confident, passionate, empowered, brave, focused, generous, loving, kind, and invested! Forgive for your own sake and ***always*** be humble enough to apologize when you're in the wrong!

Think: *Who do I wanna be, and how do I wanna be seen?*

Want It, Don't Need It

Don't be desperate—desperation is a negative emotion that doesn't serve you positively. *So, when it comes to your goals and intentions, want it but don't need it!*

Confidence Is Key

Avoid frustration—believe that what you desire is already unfolding in your favor.

Face the Past to Move Forward Fast

Address negative memories and reframe them for growth and reduced stress. Use them to strengthen and uplift yourself.

Live With Intention:

- *Be excited* for opportunities, embrace challenges, and focus on what you want to achieve—every single day!
- *Create your own "good luck"* by aligning your actions with your goals—never contradicting your intent with self-sabotaging choices!
- Because you're a kind, positive, community-based person, you're never arrogant, only positively confident!
- Approach every day as if it's your best—not your last!

Give to Receive

Share love, knowledge, and kindness with positive intent—you'll receive it back in abundance!

Moderation is Key

Less is more. Simplicity fosters greater appreciation and balance. We need far less than we think to live happily and thrive. When we strip away excess—whether in consumption, commitments, or even thoughts—we make space for what truly matters. Moderation isn't deprivation; it's about refining your life to include more of the things that nourish your mind, body, and soul!

Be the First to Greet

Approach others with warmth and positivity—you'll be remembered for all the right reasons. Be excited to see, spend time with, and share in others' enjoyment so that they'll want to engage in yours as well! ***Remember:*** *Give to receive!*

Stay Organized

Clear your mind by writing down tasks to reduce the stress of worry or forgetfulness. Focus on one thing at a time and savor the satisfaction of *gettin' shit done!*

Think and Look Positively

Overshadow negativity with positive thinking and a smile. A smile and an optimistic attitude can change your mindset and your whole world!

Mirror Your Surroundings Accordingly

Surround yourself with people who inspire and uplift you—and be a source of positivity for others too!

Celebrate Others and Their Achievements

Instead of slowing down someone else's success, help accelerate it—because a better you, plus a better me, equals a better we! *←Sounds cheesy, I know—but it's true!*

Play to Win and Live With Joy

Life isn't about avoiding loss—it's about playing to win and having fun while doing it–*'cause you want it—you don't need it, remember?!* Learn from your losses, celebrate your accomplishments, cherish your relationships, and contribute positively to your community to live happily!

Choose Consciously

Your choices in what you eat, drink, and breathe—how you rest and exercise, and what you think (project), determine the health of your personal energy field, the health of your body, and ultimately the level of happiness and success you achieve. So, be *Accountable* and positive about your problem-solving abilities, and be consciously *Aware* of and satisfied with your *Lifestyle choices!*

Summary—Lifestyle Blueprint:

- **Mindset:** Keep positive thoughts at the forefront and gently defuse negativity in the background.
- **Emotional Balance:** Release suppressed emotions like anger, grief, and shame through healthy expressions to avoid continual repression and tension.
- **Accountability:** Own your role in the shaping of your reality and the outcomes of your life.
- **Self-Care:** Treat your body with care—nurture it through proper nutrition, movement, rest, and stress management.
- **Dream:** Be thankful for all you are and all you currently have while also giving your heart the chance to—*Dream Big!*
- **Be Determined:** Live, love, succeed, and enjoy!
- **Practice:** Live a balanced *Lifestyle Philosophy* that continually integrates and builds upon all the above!

Conclusion

Your *Lifestyle Philosophy* is your compass, and whether you know it or not, you're already living one right now—and there's nothing wrong with you or your approach to life unless it's not serving you the way you like!

With a positive, confident, and resilient *Lifestyle Philosophy*, you'll not only protect your well-being but also attract the life you desire. A positive attitude, supported by positive lifestyle habits, aligns you with the *Law of Attraction* and the *Mind & Body Connection* theory, empowering you to realize your dreams and achieve your very best health, *Responsibly!*

Success is available to everyone, at any age, no matter where you are, no matter what you've been doing up to this point. Control is available to you–you just have to be aware of it, to own it.

Remember: *Positive Surround, Positive Within, Positive Out—for a Positive Rebound—it's just that simple!*

Wisdom Review

The *Wisdom Review* serves as a way to further ingrain the principles you have reviewed and, in turn, further their positive influence on your life. Within these pages, you'll find transformative insights and practical wisdom designed to empower you with knowledge, lifestyle practices, and inspiration to help you realize your highest potential!

This section distills the essence of self-awareness, intentional living, and personal evolution, reinforcing the key philosophies that shape a life of harmony, abundance, and well-being. Let each insight serve as a stepping stone toward a deeper understanding of all you've reviewed so far.

Embrace this wisdom. *Live it. Grow by it.*

All who receive such knowledge and believe are completely worthy—no one more than another, quite honestly.

Universal and Medical Facts

No Better. No Worse.
The principles herein are relevant to all of us. When it comes to our needs and desires, we're more alike than not. Furthermore, our lives start and end the very same—we only differ by where, when, to whom, and by a name—none of which, as individuals, do we have a say! Think about those facts the next time you choose to hate or judge another... Should they do the same back? *Love and hate as you choose, but do so with reason—not shallow, preconceived notions!*

Bodily Functionality
The nervous system is influenced by your emotions, and in turn, the nervous system influences your immune system. This affects the course of disease control within the body. The immune system is there to provide the healthiest, most protected version of yourself. So, support your body, which is there to support your life and the length thereof!

Stress
Any stress, including drinking, eating, and having negative thoughts and intense negative emotions, interferes with the body's healing, rebuilding, and prevention (anti-aging) process. So, all stress must be *short-lived!*

Thoughts, Emotions, Beliefs

Your Choice
Where you're from is not who you are—unless you allow it to be.

You're Not a Victim
You have more control over your circumstances and your future than you may have acknowledged in the past—until now. Your conscious choices of what you eat, drink, breathe, and otherwise take in; how you react to life's daily challenges; the quality of rest you achieve; your exercise routine (or lack thereof); the nouns that surround you (people, places, things); your beliefs; and the energy you project (your thoughts) all contribute to the health and success you experience. The health of your body, your physical pain level, your happiness, and the reality you attract (whether consciously or not) depend on the choices you make, inside and out, today and forever—just like they always have and always will! *So, awareness for such is a must!*

The Many Forms of Stress
Your body must respond to everything you put in it: food, drinks, drugs, and thoughts. Common physical stress, like working out or having a meal, can be considered short-term and thus, normal and harmless. Constant emotional stress and the stress from bad lifestyle habits is more *long-term* and very taxing on your mind

and body, potentially leading to physical pain, ill health, and quite possibly, an undesirable reality that unfolds right in front of you, as your life.

Mind & Body: Aging
Emotional stress can factor in and influence the course of autoimmune disease and cancer formation in the human body. Positive emotions do the exact opposite!

Internal Health
When your body's free of heavy stress, your immune system is repairing your body and properly handling invaders, like common viruses and even cancerous cells. *You should* now see the benefit of keeping your body in a low-stress, positive state as much as possible. That's the point of mindfulness and self-care: *positive in and positive out to defend against the rot!*

Claim Your Inner Negativity to Help Boost Your Immunity
The perfect background mind knows everything going on in and about the body and uses all its abilities to accomplish one thing: survival—survival now, at all costs. Be aware of this medical truth and make it work (less often) for you! Keep the survival mode for emergencies only by keeping stress, in all its many forms, *short-lived!*

Universal Truth: Relevant to All
Don't confuse chance, genetics, diet, and exercise alone as the sole contributing factors. It's the **complete** mindset and lifestyle routine that has greatly helped develop what is seen for you and for me.

Face the Truth with a Positive Approach
You can't change the unchangeable; however, you can make the most of it!

Aging
We let ourselves grow older, not only by design but also by neglect. We are the result of the stress imposed on our minds and on our bodies. Such a reality can be reversed to a degree with improved lifestyle habits and *Baggage Claiming!*

Long-Term Stress, the Problem Child!
Stressful thinking and stressful emotions affect your whole world—including the hair on your head—the amount and even its color! Long-term stress also impacts the health of your heart and your immune system's ability to fight off illnesses! Stress can even affect the way you walk due to stress-induced lower back pain! *Stress! Ugh... WTH!*

Positive Emotions—Your Best Choices!
Love and gratitude are the most positive—most powerful of all emotions. So love and be grateful for everything!

Harmful Emotions—The Ones to Avoid!

Low self-worth and rage, in all their many forms, are the most damaging of all emotions. So, kick that crap to the curb!

Universal Truth

It's impossible to feel bad when you're having good thoughts and focusing on being glad—because that would defy all sound logic!

Beliefs Can Evolve!

Your whole life—everything you know or believe—has been taught or learned. However, that doesn't necessarily mean that what you believe is proven, valid, or even healthy for you to keep. In life, if something doesn't feel right, it probably isn't. Open your mind's eye instead of living blind because the truth could be more heart-healthy and well worth your time!

Beliefs Can Be Invalid and Ill-Serving

Beliefs may be bogus, but they're always true to the believer and your beliefs are true to you. There are three types of beliefs that are especially devastating to your health, happiness, and your success: the belief of not being worthy, the belief that you can't achieve, and the belief that you are not loved or wanted. These are universally accepted as being *bogus-ass beliefs*—and now that you know better, there's no further need in ever believing bogusly!

Evolving Truths

If your beliefs don't fit, change 'em—change 'em the same way they were formed. Start with a thought—a new belief, accompanied by a strong feeling of validation and faith. Believe it to be true and feel dang good about it! Use this exercise to update your feelings about yourself and your abilities. *Your thoughts reflect your beliefs, and your reality reflects your thinking. So, believe and think positively about everything!*

Suppression & Traumatic Life Experiences

Accumulation of Stress

Internal rage can develop at an early age, often rooted in not feeling good enough, a belief shaped by what we hear from others. Rage can also emerge after the loss of a loved one, where feelings of abandonment arise from the loss. Intense grief can manifest as a broken heart after the loss of a loved one as well. Rage and resentment can develop from an unhealthy relationship, where the return on investment doesn't meet expectations. Rage can build due to the pressures of everyday life, especially when you feel overwhelmed or without the ability to experience the freedom to do as you please. No matter the type of repressed emotion, you need to think about what the heck you're doin' and what *you must* do to make it better—for you! *Be aware of your baggage and claim it! Make a lifestyle change to keep it less intense!*

An Environment Can Ill-Serve

Emotional distress often stems from upbringing or conditioning—like the belief that children should be seen, not heard, or rigid notions of right and wrong, whether religious or otherwise. This also applies to children of parents battling alcoholism, drug addiction, depression, or anxiety. Such experiences can leave lasting trauma until one gains awareness of suppressed emotions like rage or low self-worth and how they hinder growth. If this resonates, acknowledge your inner baggage—what it is, why it exists, who's involved, and why it must be addressed. Seek help to release suppressed emotions through constructive conversations and healthy, expressive activities—and please, consistently practice such a positive lifestyle routine for lasting progress! Remember, a design is only as good as its upkeep. If you repair or improve any area of your life but don't maintain it, then you've ultimately accomplished nothing—at least nothing that will last!

The Little Truck That No Longer Could

Anger can start and accumulate from childhood. Like the collection of junk in a truck bed, such accumulation can last a lifetime and can eventually weigh you down and bring you to a screeching halt. This can result in physical pain and/or an eruption of some sort—both of which are undesirable and can rob you of the life you'd rather be living. Such intense inner negativity can be sensed when you cannot explain why you suffer from chronic pain or chronic fatigue—or why you feel sad, depressed, uninterested, uneasy, or unable to properly rest. Clean out that ol' truck with your "*Baggage Claim*" technique found herein, so that you can more easily roll on again!

Pressure Cooker

An unrealistic self-image can put pressure on you because it is unreasonable to expect such a level of perfection or goodness without fault or criticism. In such a case, negative emotions of failure are likely to be repressed and will need to be addressed with awareness and a valid perception.

Traumatic Life Events Are Often Precursors to Illness

Ever heard of death from a broken heart? It's hard to say whether you'll end up with cancer, cardiovascular disease, autoimmune disease, or chronic pain when dealing with intense emotions like grief, anger, rage, resentment, low self-worth, humiliation, shame, or continual frustration. Either way, such prolonged intense negativity will eventually affect you negatively. To reverse or ease these conditions, use therapy and self-awareness to identify the repressed intense emotions your background mind is dealing with and likely trying to shield your conscious mind from. Then, work to release your symptoms through healthy activities and constructive expressions. *You will start to feel better—but you must keep it up!*

You Can't Dance and Stay Uptight!

Exercise vents emotions externally and uses the adrenaline associated with negative emotions, effectively relieving internal pressure! *So don't stay uptight—move your body when you're hurting emotionally!*

Life After Bad Stuff

You *can* live a meaningful, enjoyable life after trauma, because you belong to! But it's up to you. Sometimes, the desire to heal must be powerful. Reading this book and applying its principles shows your commitment. Seeking professional help when needed proves you're willing to do whatever it takes to move beyond your baggage, and that level of determination is something to be damn proud of!

Psychogenic Pain and the Shift in Focus

Something You Need to Be Aware Of

Psychogenic pain is physical pain triggered or worsened by psychological factors like stress, anxiety, depression, or unresolved emotional issues tied to memories. Although stress-induced pain isn't caused by a visible injury, it's real and can severely affect quality of life, manifesting as tension headaches, neck or lower back pain, muscle aches, or stomach issues. Effective treatment involves addressing the underlying psychological factors through self-awareness, honesty, therapy, stress management, and lifestyle changes—not cover-ups or quick fixes! *Note: memories can be relived due to their intensity or impact on your conscious mind, or by the repetitive nature of your current life, causing the associated emotions to resurface just as profoundly at times as the very day the memory was actually lived!*

Ease Psychogenic Pain

Awareness has a powerful therapeutic effect on easing or eliminating psychogenic pain. When you consciously recognize this pain as harmless and as a diversion tactic of the background mind to prevent overwhelming emotional distress, you can then address it more effectively. Stress induced physical pain results from the background depriving an area of oxygen, creating discomfort to distract the conscious mind from unresolved emotional pain, as the conscious mind handles physical pain better than ongoing emotional agony. Our mindset is essential for health and survival, so we can become diverted consciously without noticing it or having control over the transition, initially. If you experience unexplained physical pain, combat it by cultivating awareness and setting the intent to resolve the inner negativity beneath the surface. Ask yourself: What, why, and who's involved with my inner negativity? Acknowledge all it's doing to and taking from you. Then ask: How can I learn, forgive, be thankful, and improve, allowing me to move on for good?

Recognize Psychogenic Pain

When you feel non-medically induced or unexplained pain, ask yourself: What's happening in my life, and why does my background mind prefer causing physical pain over facing emotional pain consciously? Why are my emotions so intense or negative that they drag me down? Speak or even shout at your background mind for doing this—the pain may lessen or vanish. Acknowledge that you understand its tactic; the pain is harmless and exists only to distract you from painful memories and suppressed emotions. Tell your background mind that you will no longer be diverted from confronting your inner negativity—because you can handle it! You can even instruct it to increase blood flow to the pain area, providing more oxygen and relieving discomfort. Then, actively address and process the true reasons for your inner emotional baggage—don't let it weigh you down any longer!

Note: The goal is to live in a positive, low-stress state. What stands in our way are our emotions, beliefs, and attitude—shaped by memories, life experiences, upbringing, surroundings, and our own reasoning. ***Ultimately, you can choose your mindset!*** Awareness, personal accountability, and a supportive lifestyle grant you a great amount of control over your life—inside and out—regardless of what comes your way!

Baggage Claim

The Hard Truth
A lot of life is about acceptance—so accept everything around you for what it is, why it is, and why you can't change it, and you'll be so much better off you did!

A Transmission Has Reverse for a Reason
Sometimes ya gotta go back to move forward. Address your negative emotions from a nagging memory: learn a lesson, practice forgiveness (for your own sake), and be thankful for the insights gained. Be grateful that the event is over and take comfort in knowing that you may never have to experience that heartache again—at least not to the same extent. Why? *Because now, you're more aware, in-control, and thus—more resilient!*

Personal Growth
By viewing and experiencing life as a series of lessons to be learned, you come to understand that *you can't really fail at anything*. Rather, you're free to learn, grow, and develop the resilient ability necessary to move on continually!

Gut Check—Are You a Tough Ass?
Failure is nothing more than dedication validation. Failure in life is inevitable—what you do afterward isn't.

You and I Both
Aware and accountable people don't blame anyone—not even themselves. Accountable people, like you and me, accept, learn, forgive, give thanks, and move the heck on, whenever stuff goes wrong!

The Harsh Truth
Make no mistake—*no one cares about the excuses you make*. It's the results that make 'em talk!

Next Up, Please!

Yesterday's memories color today's health. Yesterday's experiences are over, finished, done. You can't do anything about what's already happened, so don't allow what's already happened to continually happen to you!

How to Defuse a Bomb!

You can't erase a negative memory, nor can you convert a negative emotion into a positive one. However, you can defuse inner negativity through acceptance and gratitude for surviving the negative event and learning a lesson from it. Finally, finding satisfaction in your conclusion leaves no reason for a negative memory to continually bother you, and its associated negative emotions will have lost their power too!

Forgiveness is "Me-Centered"

Forgive for your own sake. To forgive does not mean to approve. You don't forgive to make someone else feel better—you forgive initially for YOU. Either way, if you want the best internal operating environment for your body, whenever you're hurt or upset, you must forgive all involved—including yourself!

Empowerment to Take Control

It's OK to acknowledge, forgive, and to set the record straight. It's OK to let 'em know that you've made peace but that—that crap won't ever fly again! After all, it's your life and your right to let 'em know that *you chose* to let it go, because *you're empowered to choose* and to do so! You're now taking control—and soon, everyone around you will know it to be true!

Owning Your Role to Help You Move On

Apologizing and taking ownership of your role in things is a powerful act—it takes more guts than avoidance. So, be proud of yourself for doing it and *meaning it!*

Accountability

The Cover-Up

Medications or drugs aren't the answer to handling stress or physical pain, as they require continual use and are short-term solutions. Instead, treat the root cause for a more long-term resolution and greater independence gained!

What's Your Age Again?

When you become an adult, you can no longer blame your baggage on someone else. After all, even if you're right in pointing the finger, what does that really do for you? Be aware, be accountable, learn, forgive, and make it better—for you! No matter how you play it, no matter what you think, only you suffer from your own reality. Focus on the present and your desired future, 'cause nothing else really matters— *unless you allow it to!*

Accountability

You're not entitled to or deserving of anything; rather, it's all up to you to choose, to do, and to prove—all your good fortunes to come true!

You and You Alone

Your health and happiness are no one else's responsibility—it's up to you and you alone. So, stand up for yourself and against anyone or anything that gets in the way of your happiness and good health—*even if that someone or something is yourself!*

Discover a Better Way

Sacrificing your happiness for someone else is unfathomable. Rather, we should support and complement each other in our individual quest for the best life imaginable!

Your Mindset

Some think "outside the box" but the real skill at times is succeeding while "inside the box!" Instead of negatively focusing on what you lack and making excuses for it, which is a waste of time, rather, be thankful for and maximize what you currently have to meet your needs. Dream and work appropriately toward the reality you'd rather have while being positive for all you *do* currently have. Even if all you have is the air you breathe—that's enough to live your day! And if you have a day to live, then that's a chance to give your *Inner Genius* the opportunity to figure out a better way toward a better existence! The real talent at times is the ability to thrive while trapped "inside the box." After all, you can't make chicken soup from chicken poop… but you can, however, grow a heck of a garden with it!

Note: Don't just stand around talkin' about how it could be or how it should be. Take action and make it a reality!

Be More Than Good Enough

There's always a barrier of some kind that we must overcome, and often it's something we have no control over. So instead of focusing on the barrier itself and making excuses about it, work to become so good that you'll succeed, no matter how many barriers you have to blow through to proceed!

The Ultimate Problem-Solving Routine

Talk to and advise yourself as if you were talking to and advising someone else. You already have mostly all the right answers, or at least, when given a chance to think, you have the right starting point and attitude in mind! So, talk it out—listen to the wise one within you and take your own advice, why don't ya!

Ease Contradictory Thinking

Argue against the choices you make just as much as you argue to justify them in the first place. Then, be honest with yourself—which case sounds better? Make sure you're not contradicting your current goals and ultimate dream with your decisions!

Lifestyle

Whenever you see someone else happy—*don't be jelly; go get your own and fill your own belly!*

Universal Truth

The air we breathe and the chance to live, really might be all that is—*our birthright!*

Accountable Influence

The power of personal accountability comes from questions that begin with "what" or "how" and always contain an "I"—not "them" or "they." Worry about your own self and the impact you have on others in your life. If others around you have such awareness and good intent, they'll notice the trend, and over time, they'll follow suit. Now, that would be win-win for everyone, including you!

Self-Respect, Empowerment

Love Yourself

Even if you desire personal improvement, love and respect who and how you are at this very moment. You're free to focus on improving and achieving more but not at the expense of enjoying and being grateful for who you are now and all you currently have—'cause it could always be worse!

Monkey See, Monkey Do

You must treat yourself with love and respect before others can give you what you expect. And if you're not happy with who you are, their support won't get you far.

Words to Live By

"I am" are the two most powerful words, so use them wisely. Follow them with the most positive adjectives and the most positive intent you can muster! Repeat after me: "I am a great person, and I am completely capable and worthy of achieving a great, enjoyable, fulfilling, and pain-free life!"

Universal Truth

The human spirit knows that it can do anything; however, it's the conscious mind that is fearful and lacks the confidence and motivation necessary to *"go for it"* at times. Shut that kinda thinkin' down and build yourself up—now!

Lifestyle

Your daily life and your career should be approached as a chance to embrace, learn, improve, impress, evolve, and enjoy! If you truly approach your day in such a way, you'll happily succeed—over and over, again and again!

Don't Front—Put Your Big Pants On and Own Your Junk

You're not perfect and don't always have it under control. Don't hide or be ashamed of your inner baggage and imperfections. Instead, recognize 'em, own 'em, embrace 'em, show no shame for 'em, and work on the ones that are most bothersome. Everyone around you will respect and relate to you—'cause everybody has *stuff*—and everyone's already aware of yours—just like you are of theirs!

Start to Reinvent Yourself—In 5 Minutes!

Reflect on your perceived faults, mistakes, and limiting beliefs. Acknowledge their influence on your past and accept these as part of an old reality—something that's shaped you in the past but will no longer define you from now on. Now, forgive yourself and consciously decide to let go. Take a moment—close your eyes—imagine your ideal self—the person you dream of being. Think of that image and ask yourself: How do they act, think, feel, and engage with the world? Visualize these qualities in detail. Now, create a vivid, inspiring image of the *current you* stepping into this *improved version of yourself.* With this vision in mind, consciously align your thoughts and actions to reflect this transformation. Each decision, no matter how small, is an opportunity for you to reinforce your growth. Speak, move, and live as the new and improved you, as if it's already your truth—because, in a sense, it is, and it will continue to remain so for as long as you practice and believe it to be so!
Remember: Practice for it, 'til you make it—legit!

Love Who You Are

Accept and love who you are now, especially the things you cannot change. Get excited about the things you can change and all the things you can dream of and achieve! Although we all suffer from limitations, there's still so much we can improve on, starting with our conscious mindset! No matter what the area of life, as long as we have the time and the desire, we can all dream and practice for our very highest potential—because as humans, therein lies our true power!

Relationships

Potential Poison

Your attitude is infectious. So think about what you intend to spread—*and own it!*

Living Among Others

If you're not happy within, then confrontation can easily begin.

Note: If your attitude wears *you* down emotionally, then what do you think your attitude does to *everybody!*

Acceptance

You can't please or change others, so don't try. Never let their actions dictate your happiness or stir rage or resentment within you. Instead, change how they affect you by understanding who they are and why they are the way they are—choose to forgive and accept them as they are. Express your feelings constructively and propose reasonable resolutions. If that's not enough, for your own peace of mind, change your surroundings! *Ultimately, it's on you and it's your right to choose, because, at the end of the day, **you're the only reason why you truly win or lose.***

Set Things Straight for Your Own Sake!

If you're unhappy with how things are going in your life, especially in a certain relationship, don't hesitate to speak up. The truth may hurt, but people will get over it. Pain is inevitable—whether short-term from expressing the truth or long-term from suppressing negative feelings and general unhappiness. If this resonates with you, then you have two options for the pain you'll have to endure: short-term or long-term. *Now, which one can you afford?!*

Express Yourself

Express your intentions and your goals with all those you're sharing a life with. Constructive, calm conversation, is the one clear way of "getting on the same page." After all, you can't get what you want if no one knows about it—*and when it comes to your feelings and needs, they'll either be expressed or repressed! Now, which action do you think serves you best?!*

Be Heard, Not Ignored

At times, your approach can stink even though your intent is pure and your purpose is important to you. You may believe your heart is in the right place, but your message gets lost in fussy translation as a result of messy conversation. We all fall victim to our emotions at times, especially in heated debate. However, exhibit self-awareness, positive intention, and work toward improvement. Aways try and express yourself constructively and respectfully so that your intentions and feelings are heard —not ignored!

Express to Avoid Regret—But Keep Yourself In-Check!

If something needs to be resolved, be mindful of the right time, the right place, and the right way to say what's on your mind to get stuff straight!

Attract More with Honey

Don't just stand up for how you feel when it's bothersome—also remember to express how you feel when it's positive! You should tell the ones you value and love how and why you feel positively about them more often! It does your heart good and theirs also! After all, who's gonna turn away from a pure, loving thought or kind compliment? *NO ONE AT ALL! And who knows what you'll get in return!*

A Need for Emissions Check Testing

If you're depressed, angry, or unhappy in general, your whole body responds in an unfavorable, negative manner. However, if you adopt a confident, cheerful, and positive outlook, such an attitude triggers a more favorable, positive, whole-body response! Focus on spending more of your daily life being positive than otherwise. To achieve our best health and the dreams we hold dear, we must strive to remain in a low-stress, positive state as much as we possibly can. But life happens, and your mind tends to wander. So, make a point to practice the *"Emissions Check"* test, up next, throughout your day to align your thinking appropriately.

The Emissions Check Test

Whenever you feel a sense of negative energy, course-correct with accountable thinking. Ask yourself: Why am I feeling negative? What do I need to do to make it better? Exercise perspective—is it worth it? Likely not, so let it go and refocus on something more positive, like your goals and all the things you hold dear, like loved ones! *Align yourself with your intended path—a more positive one—STAT!*

Avoid Negativity

Save Your Fight for a Real Fight!

Don't get sucked into someone else's shenanigans or negativity. We've all been involved in a petty, negative situation. A common example is an aggressive, angry driver. Steer clear and don't engage, and don't allow them to negatively affect you. Because someone else's ugliness is theirs... and for your sake, it needs to stay that way!

Don't Dirty Ya Shoes

If you're trying to be a good person and others don't treat you the same, that's their problem! Don't get pulled down to their level and walk around in their shit! Better yet, change how the outside world affects you and if that doesn't work, change your negative surroundings! Either way, never hesitate to seek help in accomplishing this!

I Second That!

"F" hatred. Agreed?!

How We *Should* Think

To hell with evilness—that's the only place it belongs!

Law of Attraction

Don't talk about or focus on other people's downfalls, especially to make yourself feel better. Do you really want to feel better at someone else's expense? It's more likely that you'll receive a negative response by focusing on someone else's negative junk. *So think twice when you wanna think dumb!*

The Nouns That Surround (People, Places, and Things)

If you listen to doom and gloom, then you too will become doom and gloom. As the ol' sayin' goes, *"Birds of a feather flock together."* So, choose wisely who and what surrounds you, 'cause it makes a difference!

Positivity Over Negativity

Your positive emotions should double your current negative ones. You can't always totally defuse or eliminate your inner negativity but you can, however, overshadow negativity with positivity. Think of it like a water hose—*drown out negative power with a positive water shower.*

The Law of Attraction & Empowerment

Level Playing Field
Some people naturally embrace their visions and just let 'em unfold, but whether it comes easily or not, we're all influenced by the same universal truths—the Law of Attraction, the Mind-Body Connection theory, our level of personal Accountability, our Lifestyle Philosophy, and, most importantly, our level of Awareness for all of it! What you do with this knowledge and how it shapes your life is entirely up to you— *just as it always has been—just as it always will be!*

How Exciting Is It to Think—If They Can...
If Jeff, Bill, Mark, Melanie, Whitney, and Ms. Winfrey can, then why the heck not you and me—at least to some satisfactory degree?!

Note: Not much happens "over-night." It's a marathon, so it has to be a lifestyle!

Achiever's Attitude
Don't say, "I can't." Instead, if it matters to you, say, "How can I?"

Use The Law of Attraction for Your Benefit
Whether it's positivity or negativity, you attract what you focus on most. So, by maintaining clear intentions, positive thoughts, and complementary actions, *you can draw desired experiences and outcomes into your life as a direct reaction!*

Dream Away—But Don't Just Wait for It, Practice for It!
You're free to dream up the darndest of "positive" things, but you must also routinely practice for it. No matter what it is you wish to receive, you can achieve— at least to some satisfactory degree! So, dream, *practice for*, and believe in all the wonderful things you wish to see!

Your World Is Only a Mirror of You and Your Actions!
Give love to receive love. Give money to receive prosperity. Share the knowledge you have to help improve someone else's position so that you too, may grow in wealth of worth and wisdom!

Give For the Right Reason!
Live a lifestyle of giving for the joy of giving and not solely for receiving. Otherwise, doing so with the wrong mindset places your heart in the wrong place, and the energy you emit reflects the same. **Remember:** *The actions of your true intent will ultimately determine what you get.* So, give only with positive intent—so that you only receive positivity for doing it!

Don't Be an ASS!
There's never a need in being mean. No matter who you're dealing with, what you emit, you shall surely get. And when it comes to being mean, you'll only attract *shit!*

Law of Attraction
The act of judging someone is negative, and you know what happens next...

Lifestyle
Gossip is often a negative act, as it usually comes at someone else's expense. Discussing someone who isn't present, makes it very likely to be unkind and unproductive. While it may offer entertainment, it's cheap and shallow. If you're gonna talk about someone, let it be with the intent to support, uplift, or be there for them—something more akin to *praying for,* rather than, *gossiping about!*

Law of Attraction
What you *worry* over, you bring over. And without a doubt, what you *stress* about, you bring about.

Next-Level Stuff
Learn to love the things you hate—'cause that kinda strength's gonna make you great!

No Oxymorons Here
You can't have a negative mindset if you're thinking positively—and you can't have a frown on your face if instead, you have a smile in its place. *Facts!*

No Oxymoron Here Either
You can't have a positive frame of mind if you're engaged with negativity. *So, be aware of the nouns that surround and be accountable for your constant thinking!*

Empowerment
When you take control of your life, *only you can make yourself happy or mad.*

Win the Battle—One Day at a Time!
Every day is a fresh start and a new chance to win the day with success over our temptations, bad lifestyle habits, and whatever else is in the way of our personal achievements. No matter who you are, we all have to work at being the person we intend to be and practice for all we intend to receive. Over time, our routine becomes more second nature, but we must remain mindful and continually practice appropriately, nevertheless. And make no mistake, yesterday's gone, so let it be and let it go. *Now get motivated to succeed and get over your stuff. Your fresh start begins the same as everyone else—12 AM on the dot!*

We Work for the Heart Whom Works for Us Back!

Changing your life status is nearly impossible without awareness, and the same applies to addictions like shopping, gambling, smoking, drugs, or dieting—attempts to fill a void that discipline alone cannot cure. True change requires awareness of the need for inner spiritual and emotional work, along with honest recognition of where you are now and where you want to be. Practice awareness to identify the source of your void and fill it with something more concrete, like family or goal-oriented activities. Most importantly, be gentle with yourself—embrace who you are now and let that self-love fuel your motivation to improve, just as your heart desires! *Because with mindful ways and actions true, your heart's desire stays with you. Through practice clear and vision bright, your dreams will never fade from sight!*

Someone Wants to Help

Never resist or hesitate when it comes to receiving professional care. There are professionals out there whose dream it is to help people like you and me. So, why not help their dreams come true while they're helping make the same happen for you?!

Self-Awareness—A Real Game Changer

There are so many things in life that are ultimately beyond our control. However, with the power of conscious awareness for the effects of positive thinking, and awareness of the vivid dream that lives in your heart, you begin to realize that you're more capable than you likely ever thought!

If Your Life's Not Goin' the Way You Like—Think and Act

Think: Do my actions align with my intent, and is my intent positive? **Act:** Consult with your Inner Genius for directive, and change your mindset for a more favorable existence!

It's Your Time, Baby!

The Secret Gift is—The Power of Thought! So practice Life's most valuable Loophole—*Awareness* to unlock the potential of your Secret Gift! Think it, believe it, live it, and be thankful for it to see it become legit!

Plenty of Goodness Out There for All of Us

Never seek success at the direct expense of someone else. If your intention involves harming others for your own gain, then you're undermining your own pursuit of genuine success and happiness! If your motivation is rooted in the desire to see others falter, then you're inviting negativity into your own journey. Life often involves surpassing others, but this should never stem from ill will. *Either way, in victory or loss, focus only on the positive!*

Don't Count Your Chickens Before They Hatch

Want it, but don't need it. Avoid the emotions of neediness or desperation as they are negative energies. Be confident that you will receive what you desire, and better yet, have faith that it's already forming right before your eyes—because you're also practicing for it too, right?! Allow it to manifest in its own way—'cause that's the journey! Learn to embrace and enjoy the ride toward the vision you hold dear in your mind's eye!

What You Daydream, You Can Bring–To Real Life!
When you can't physically act, mentally act. Your background mind doesn't know the difference between having done something or having dreamed it. Whether it's a vision or a memory replayed, your background mind believes your visions are real, especially when there's real emotion attached (make it positive here). Either way, your constant visions become second nature—so, make sure your visions work in your favor! *Daydream it, 'til you make it legit!*

Be Patient
Enjoy setting goals and focusing on the bigger picture—your dream—but don't concern yourself with the details such as who, where, when, or how. Instead, focus on the "what"—the goal or dream itself—and the "why"—why it's important to you. The details are in the journey. *Give the journey a chance to play out. Focus only on the dream and don't let the positive energy toward it flame out!*

Give it Time
Go with the flow. It will all work out in its own time—if that's what you truly desire and practice for, all the while.

Reality, Perspective

Universal Truth
Make the very most of every day, because someday will be your very last day. Think about that and tell me if that doesn't wake your ass up!

Lifestyle
Don't wait for the right time—make *now* the right time!

Priorities: You Can't Do Anything 100% of the Time
Is the vision you dream worth all that it takes to make it come true? Make sure your dreams and goals in life are worth everything required to bring them to life. Awareness, accountability, focus, and a complementary daily routine is the recipe for achieving all the good things you intend to receive. The daily practice is the one ingredient that varies from dream to dream—so, make sure you're not neglecting what matters most or spreading yourself too thin! ***Put simply, make sure the juice is worth the squeeze!***

The Grass Over Yonder Might Be Greener
Some people seek a beautiful place, while others make a place beautiful right where they stand! The grass under your feet *could* be greener if you only nurtured and

cared for it better. With awareness, accountability, healthy expression, and positive effort, you just might gain everything you ever wanted—right where you are—without having to cross that fence and go chasin' after it, after all!

Call It for What It Is—Acknowledge a Win
Acknowledge a good day for what it is—a positive thing!

Acknowledge a Loss
Recognize a bad day for what it is—a chance to learn a lesson to further your wisdom and perspective!

A Broken Heart Will Mend
It's OK to feel. Embrace your bad days—the ones that hurt your heart the most, because that means something important to you has changed and it deserves your loving sorrow. *And although there's no timeline for healing, don't forget, you still have a life to live tomorrow.*

Help Is Not a Bad Word!
Therapy may be needed if you have strong dependency needs, conflicts over sexuality, an identity crisis, feelings of hopelessness, humiliation, or shame. These case examples typically require a licensed therapist to help reverse the process of suppression and help ease the pain. However, awareness of this is a huge first step and something you should feel extremely proud of. If this is relevant to you, please seek professional help. Meanwhile, continue reading and practicing everything you've reviewed so far because the strength's in you and *you can make it through!*

Lifestyle: Habits, Characteristics, Attitude

It's the Dose That Makes the Poison
Moderation: less is more—less hassle and more freedom to enjoy.

Lifestyle
Be dependent on less. We need far less than we think to live and to live happily.

Treat Others the Way You Wish to Be Treated
Wish for others the same things you wish for yourself. Give to receive, remember? Send good wishes instead of death kisses!

Be Top-Class
Every day—leave it better than you found it, including yourself!

Get Lucky
There's no such thing as luck—unless you desire or believe there to be. If you believe in luck, then create your own *"good"* luck, or at least avoid focusing on or talking about *"bad"* luck!

Take Action—Don't Procrastinate!

Procrastination increases stress. As things pile up, and as time goes by, you begin to feel overwhelmed or stressed by something you know you should be doing. Procrastination is a good friend of failure—so, whatever it is, start taking steps to get it done. And from now on, take care of the little things while they're still little—one routine, realistic step at a time.

Mellow Flow

Adopt a *"so what, now what"* mentality whenever life goes sideways!

Cool Head

When something *"ticks you off"* think: is it really worth all the negativity it's fueling me with? Probably not. So, instead, *"F" it*—let it go and change your mindset to dissolve any negativity in the moment.

Mellow Fellow

Choose not to engage in drama.

One with the People

Be the first to greet everyone you meet—never perch, so they don't think you're a jerk!

Lifestyle

Hug and handshake like you mean it! Don't be a dead fish when you have an opportunity to impress!

Leave a Lasting Impression

Be someone to remember, for all the right (positive) reasons.

Lifestyle

Forego hatred. Practice love... *duh*.

LOL

Laughter reduces stress, lowers adrenaline, boosts immunity, improves mood, and supports heart health by increasing blood flow and relaxation! So yes, *laughter is truly the best medicine!*

Lifestyle

Don't regret for shit!—'cause that kinda thinkin' is negative!

Mind & Body

Don't fear for shit either, especially your own—*baggage!*

You Deserve to Be Celebrated!

No matter your age, always celebrate your birthday. Ya know why? 'Cause it's your *F–in'* birthday, *and your existence deserves a celebration! You—deserve to be celebrated!* And don't forget to celebrate others, all the same!

Daily Routine

I'll Take a Lil' Coffee with My Cream and Sugar!

Be a morning person! Help yourself out by having something ready every morning that you can look forward to. Make it quick, easy, and positive, please! Get excited about it. Get excited about your morning and your positive start to a new, positive day! Start every day the exact, same, positive way! Be a morning person if you're not already, starting first thing in the AM!

At the Start of Every Day

Be accountable—always ask yourself before starting your day, "What kinda day am I gonna have?" Next, reply with something like, "A dang good one!" *Then, **practice for it!***

The Smile—The Enemy of a Frown

The power of the smile: It defuses, breaks confusion, reduces stress and anger. It impresses, it's attractive and inviting. It cultivates success and happiness and turns heads. A smile improves health and burns calories. That's how a smile serves you better than a frown! Don't believe me? Just ask around.

Brighten the Whole World

Smile to begin your day. Smile for your own sake. Smile every chance you get and never let that feeling dissipate. *Recognize and never forget: You can't wear a frown if instead you have a smile in its place, and you're never more beautiful than when you're wearin' a smilin' face!*

Try One, Every Day!

Laughter and a good cry are powerful, natural ways to release stress. While crying is often linked to emotional or physical pain and thus less desirable at times, both laughter and shedding tears serve as essential acts of emotional pressure relief—helping to restore balance. Instead of suppressing our emotions, we should embrace 'em. *So, cry and laugh your butt off more often!*

Before Sleep, Every Night

Each night, support your mind and body in their quest to repair, build up, and defend to the best of their abilities by keeping time before bed as cheerful and as positive as possible—*because, the last thoughts you have before sleeping will keep on spinning long after you've gone off dreaming!*

Sleeping Places You in Your Least Stressed State
When you properly prepare for rest, doing so with aware, positive intent, your mind and body are able to heal and protect to the height of their ability. *So remember— time taken away from quality rest, is time taken away from your personal best!*

The Wrap-Up

One Chance, One Life to Live
No matter what you believe was the beginning, or what will be the end—you and I are currently here on Earth, and we certainly won't be for long or ever again. So, why not make the most of it every day—enjoying the ride, as long as we possibly can!

Don't Abuse It. Support It. Use It for Your Own Benefit!
Your brain is the most powerful, most capable, and most diverse computer that has ever and will ever exist!… and your body's pretty magical too!

All You Really Need to Know
Have positive thoughts in the foreground portion of your mind. Defuse negative emotions in the background. Ease the pressure of your repressed and accumulated intense inner emotions. Update negative, bogus beliefs. Take *Accountability* for your involvement in your life's reality—past, present, and forever! Practice a *Lifestyle* that supports all of the above. *All made possible with your aware, in-control, influential, and determined–conscious mind!*

Universal Truth
The biggest fail—giving up on your life and the opportunity to achieve personal happiness!

You Have the Right to Live Again
There's no timeline for healing but remember, ***your life's waiting and time's ticking!***

Lifestyle
Dream and practice for tomorrow (positive); don't wait for OR try and predict it (likely negative).

Have You Lost Your Mojo?
If you feel like you've got nothing to look forward to in life, then what the hell are ya doin'? Open your eyes—open your heart, and discover something worth *"givin' a hoot about!"*

Limitations *Do* Exist
There are medical conditions and predispositions that determine our health and limitations, which cannot be influenced or improved solely by our thought process and lifestyle alone. However, no matter your predisposition, no matter your genetic

shortcomings, your goal should be to achieve your very best, happiest self for as long as you possibly can—until the very end! It has to be said aloud, because, *limitations do exist; however, you don't know what they are until they're met!*

Universal Truth

It's never too late. Even on your very last day, up until your very last breath—you still have a chance to think positively, feel happiness, and achieve inner peace—placing both your heart and mind at ease. But don't wait until then, because you have so much to look forward to, so much potential to strive for, and so much to achieve and enjoy—so don't waste another moment! You just have to believe and act to receive! *So, dream and positively practice for tomorrow—don't wait for OR try and predict it!*

Use the Feeling of Being Fed Up as a Positive Motivator

If you're tired of living in pain or underachieving, then tap into your Inner Genius and examine your habits and mindset. No matter the area of life you wish to improve, with the knowledge and resources you have, you possess the power to make real, lasting change!

Lifestyle

Approach every day as if it's your best (joyful) and not your last (stressful).

The Final Results on a Life-Long Journey

It's not about being right or wrong, good or bad. It's not about how much you didn't achieve or how much you did. Rather, it's about where you stand with yourself at the end of your days. Did you give a damn? Did you love and give yourself the opportunity to receive it back? Did you give yourself a fair chance at true happiness? *In the end, make sure you can confidently say, "Hell yes, I did!"*

Practice Section

We'll begin with our *Vision Board* to set the tone for our *Practical Lifestyle Routine*.

Then, we'll review our *Daily Mantra*, followed by a structured approach to *Emissions Checking* and *Baggage Claiming*—essential steps for maintaining awareness and emotional balance.

We'll then reinforce our journey with *Empowering Reflection*, furthering the development of our most aware, most self-serving mindset.

Finally, we'll conclude with a reflective wrap-up, bringing together the final thoughts and key insights of this book.

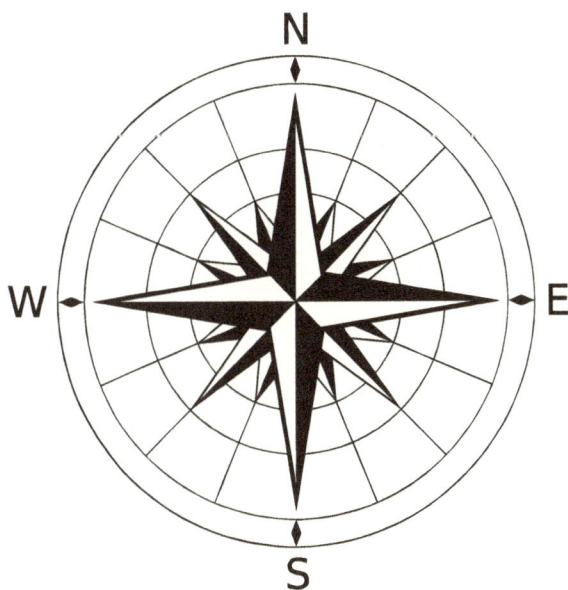

Whether it's considered a holistic or a mindful approach—it's a determined, influential, and purposeful way to go, nonetheless!

Vision Board—*(Mine)*

Document your life intentions and consult with your Inner Genius on how to achieve them. Be accountable by practicing for and revisiting them often. Seek help, where necessary! Now, get to it!

Date: *February 13, 2025*

Health—Mental & Physical	Habits to Improve on
—Drop the stubborn holiday weight. —Strengthen shoulder & reduce pain. —Focus on "smelling the roses" more often, instead of passin' 'em by! —Focus more on all the lil' things I do right, instead of all my bloopers!	—Chill with the coffee (cream & sugar). —Relax on the foul-language. —Focus on doin' laundry BEFORE Sunday afternoons! —Improve the work-life balance. —No cocktails on work nights.
Career/ Academic /Personal	**Financial & Why?**
—Afford the ability to become a "full-time" author! —Start a lil' business to enable the ability to employ & share the venture with people I'd like to empower!	—Afford the ability to retire mom & care for her-'cause she's the hardest working person I know & it's her time to relax! —Support the Mrs., in caring for her mother, 'cause that's important too!
Material Achievement	**Adventure—Places to See**
—A new car for Stacey, 'cause it's long over due-sorry hun! —A used Jeep for Dyl., 'cause he'll be gettin' his license soon! <—A project we can work on together!	—See the ocean, in Scotland! —Make NYC during the holidays to see the tree and the lights at Rockefeller! —A few computer museums & a real-live data-center. Gotta see the cloud in person!
Contributions to Community	**Things I Want to Do More Often**
—Routinely support the local youth-groups. —Look-for instead of waiting-for a sign of someone in-need. —Donate to the community kitchen. —Gonna do Secret Santa this year!	—Read, read, and read some more-'cause it's one of my most favorite things to do in the whole-wide world! —Cook, host, and spread love by gathering, sharing, and breaking bread. —Nap!!!

Relationships to Improve or Create

—Bae, we've come so far, but I'm still shriving for more outta myself, for the both of us!
—Myself-I won't let you down, at least not on purpose!
—To my crazy-ass uncle, whom I'll try harder to tolerate-but, dang man!
—Aunty-I wanna be there for ya and help ya out, however I can, but I need you to want it too! I wanna see ya have the chance to, and achieve, true happiness!

Your Vision Board: Design Your Reality!

Document your life intentions and consult with your Inner Genius on how to
achieve them. Be accountable by practicing for and revisiting them often.
Seek help, where necessary! Now, get to it!

Date:

Health — Mental & Physical	Habits to Improve on
Career/ Academic /Personal	Financial & Why?
Material Achievement	Adventure — Places to See
Contributions to Community	Things I Want to Do More Often
Relationships to Improve or Create	

A Practical Lifestyle Routine: Helping to Further Ingrain Your Values

A design is only as stable as its upkeep. Integrate the following as you see fit and commit to practicing it!

Morning
- **Be Thankful**—*Start your day with gratitude for everything, including the air you breathe and the chance to live!*
- **Have a Treat to Look Forward To**—*Give yourself something small but enjoyable—like a cup of coffee or tea!*
- **Walk** for 10 minutes while reciting your ***Daily Mantra***—*Move your body, connect spiritually, soak in the morning light, and mentally reflect on your Vision Board.*

Before You Leave and Start Your Day
- **Smile Big**—*And Mean It!*
- ***Emissions Check***—*Align your mindset with purposeful intent.*
- **Ask: What kinda day am I gonna have?** *Your Answer "A dang great one!"*

During the Day
- ***Emissions Check***—*Reassess your energy and mindset.*

Personal Time (a time or two a week)
- **Meditation & Self-Healing**—*Find strength in stillness.*
- ***Baggage Claim*** (where needed)—*Address what lingers and trust that daily mindfulness keeps negativity from taking hold.*

Evening (a few times a week)
- **Walk or jog** for 20 minutes while reciting your ***Daily Mantra*** *and mentally reflecting on your Vision Board.*

Bedtime
- **Reflect & Forgive**—*Let go of the day's weight.*
- **Give Thanks**—*End your day with gratitude, for everything!*
- **Visualize Positively**—*For Tonight & Tomorrow.*
- **Achieve Quality Sleep**—*Do what you can to achieve (4-5) hours of uninterrupted rest.*

*Detailed further soon

Daily Mantra

Michael Joseph Smith

I rose today with hope and grace,
So thankful for this time and space.

Whatever came, I made it through,
The past is done—*I've made that so.*

No matter what the future holds,
I'll make the most and let life flow.

Here today, I give my all,
This day right here is all I know.

With love and purpose guiding me,
I'm truly happy *just to be.*

Health and wealth—*they're mine to claim,*
As too are love and joy—*all the same.*

Aware of power to create,
So many *opportunities* await.

Success is mine *if I act and believe,*
Exciting my heart to *dream and receive.*

Though winds may shift and the tides may turn,
In each day, *my dreams will ever burn.*

With gratitude for *this blessed day,*
I plan to live tomorrow-the exact same way.

Emissions Check: Self Assessment

Your *Emissions Check* keeps your mind clear and your energy strong. It's a quick self-check to spot negativity, shift your focus, and stay in control. *Remember: What you constantly emit, you shall surely get!*

Whenever you're reminded to check-in, whether consciously or otherwise, don't dwell—adjust! Choose thoughts that matter more than the stress weighing you down. Negativity, no matter its form, drains both mind and body, greatly influencing your life–your reality. *Remember: You have the power to course-correct your mindset with focus and positive intent!*

When to Perform an Emissions Check:

- **Commuting** to/from work or school → Start & End the day right

- **Universe Reminder**, e.g., 10:10, 2:22, etc.

- **Feeling Off** → Check in and see what's up

- **After Social Interactions** → How did you interact, and how do you feel afterward?

- **Before Important Moments** → Check in and set your mindset

- **Downtime** → Reflect & Reset

- **Feeling Intense Pressure** → Check in and Gain Clarity

Check in, reset, move forward more positively—STAT!

Emissions Check Steps

START: With conscious awareness.
↓

HOW are you feeling?
↓

If bothersome.
↓

WHAT is it and **WHO's** involved.
↓

What's the **CAUSE**? ➡ Surroundings (reminders, stressors) or your focus in general.
↓

PERSPECTIVE ➡ Is it worth all it's doing and taking from you?
↓

Does it need further attention (Baggage Claim)? ➡ Address it more in-depth, later.
↓

ACCOUNTABILITY ➡ How can you make it better now? ➡ Then, take **ACTION**!
↓

COURSE-CORRECT ➡ Refocus on what matters most, like loved ones and goals.
↓

TAKE CONTROL ➡ Think positively and say, "negativity be damned!"
↓

FINISH: Feel dang proud of yourself! ➡ **CONTINUE** on with your day!

Baggage Claim: Deeper Healing

A lot of life is about acceptance–so accept everything around you for what and why it is, and why you can't directly change it, and you'll be so much better off for it!

Baggage Claim is a structured time for deep self-reflection—an intentional practice of confronting negativity with honesty and constructive reasoning beyond course-correcting your focus with positive thinking, such as with your *"Emissions Check"* technique. When past experiences or suppressed emotions weigh you down, this method helps you better process, resolve, and move forward by asking:

-   **Is something nagging me not easily corrected with positive thinking?** Is it my environment, past experiences, or relationships?

-   **Why does it still affect me?** How deeply does it impact my daily life?

-   **Who's involved?** Can I express myself to them? Should I repair or release this relationship?

-   **What needs to change?** Is it my perception, mindset, or surroundings that need adjustment?

-   **What's next?** Follow the *Baggage Claim* protocol and seek professional guidance if needed.

Once you've identified the root cause and those involved, embrace perception, accountability, acceptance, forgiveness, lesson-learning, and gratitude to ultimately gain confidence and satisfaction from all your hard work! *Remember: Hard work truly does pay off!*

By questioning the value of holding onto negativity, you gain clarity and motivation to release emotional baggage. This practice isn't daily but should be routine, with focused sessions no-more than 40 minutes (including expressive activity) to prevent emotional exhaustion while ensuring steady, positive progression.

Whether it's emotions tied to a negative memory or intense feelings from daily life, defuse what you can't lose (negative memories) and express what's repressed (inner intensities) with *Baggage Claiming*.

Note: When healing, never resist or feel embarrassed about seeking professional help. In today's world, support is just an app, an internet search, or a phone call away. Be aware, honest, and accountable in your approach—your actions mean everything!

Baggage Claim Steps: Be Aware, Think, Analyze, & Act

What's bothering you? A memory, beliefs, or intense emotions?

Why is it so impactful? Who's involved?

Is it worth all it's doing and all it's taking from you?

Accept its reality and seek professional help if needed.

Recognize your role in the event or in its continual influence.

Take responsibility for how you handle it moving forward.

Recognize how your environment and lifestyle affect you.

Extract lessons, even if only useful for future decisions.

Be thankful for the lessons learned and be grateful that past struggles aren't present —*if they are, change that, now!*

Forgive yourself and all others, and allow them to forgive you as well!

Make a plan to improve your situation—*for you!*

Express yourself to those involved at the right time, in the right place, and in the right way to set things straight and help ease the pain!

See your baggage as less powerful—now that you are actively addressing it, thus reducing it.

Be proud of your self-awareness and emotional resilience. Feel damn good and refocus on all you're thankful for and all you're working toward!

If Baggage is Tied to a Painful Memory:
- **Calm Your Thinking:** Walk, write, paint, sing, engage in a hobby, laugh, or spend time with loved ones who support your well-being.
- **Final Thought:** Memories should strengthen, not weaken—*so go create some positive, dang good ones!*

If Baggage is Rooted in Stress, Anger, or Frustration:
- **Physically Express:** Do cardio or sing for 20 continuous minutes to release negative energy.
- **Reclaim Calm:** Use meditation, deep breathing, prayer, journaling, or visualization.
- **Final Thought:** Your emotions shape your health and how others see you—**so ask yourself:** Who do I wanna be, and how do I wanna be seen?

EMPOWERING REFLECTION

IT'S HARD TO FEEL REJECTED, UNACCEPTED, OR NEGLECTED
WHEN YOU'RE FOCUSED ON GIVING THANKS FOR A BLESSING.

IT'S HARD TO GROW TIRED WITH SO MUCH OF THE WORLD AROUND,
HERE TO INSPIRE.

IT'S HARD TO FEEL SELF-DOUBT WHEN YOU'RE TAKING A MORE
EMPOWERED ROUTE.

IT'S SILLY TO COMPARE YOUR STORY TO OTHERS, NOR IS IT YOUR
BUSINESS TO WORRY ABOUT ANOTHER.

YOU WON'T FEEL ENTITLED OR DESERVING WHEN YOU HAVE AN
ATTITUDE FOR FURTHER LEARNING.

YOU CAN'T FEEL HOPELESS WHEN YOU ARE LASER-FOCUSED.

YOU CAN'T BE UNDERVALUED IF EVERY DAY YOU'RE DRIVEN TO
POSITIVELY CONTRIBUTE.

YOU CAN'T HAVE LOW SELF-WORTH WITH POSITIVE EFFORT.

HOW CAN YOU NOT BE CAPABLE OR GOOD ENOUGH, BUT YET—
EVERYONE ELSE?

HOW CAN YOU BE LESSER OR BETTER WHEN WE'RE ALL HERE
TOGETHER?

OUR STORIES ALL START AND END THE VERY SAME; ONLY WHEN,
WHERE, TO WHOM, AND A NAME SEPARATE EACH MAN.

HOW CAN YOU INTEND TO HARM ANOTHER WHEN IT FEELS SO MUCH
BETTER BEING A FRIEND OR A LOVER?

YOU CAN'T BE A FOLLOWER OF A CREW WHEN YOU'RE IN CHARGE
OF-YOU!

HOW CAN YOU NOT RECEIVE LOVE IN RETURN IF YOU'RE GIVING
IT AT EVERY TURN?

YOU CAN'T HAVE A NEGATIVE MINDSET IF YOU'RE THINKING POSITIVELY.

YOU CAN'T HAVE A FROWN ON YOUR FACE IF INSTEAD YOU'RE WEARIN' A SMILE IN ITS PLACE.

IT'S IMPOSSIBLE TO FEEL UNGRATEFUL OR MAD, WHEN YOU'RE FOCUSED ON BEING GLAD FOR ALL YOU CURRENTLY HAVE.

FOCUSING ON WHAT YOU DON'T HAVE IS A WASTE OF TIME AND ENERGY—NEITHER OF WHICH YOU'LL EVER GET BACK.

MAKE NO MISTAKE, NO ONE CARES ABOUT THE EXCUSES YOU MAKE. IT'S THE RESULTS THAT MAKE 'EM TALK!

THE AIR TO BREATHE AND A CHANCE TO LIVE, REALLY MIGHT BE ALL THAT IS—OUR BIRTHRIGHT!

YOU CAN'T EASILY FAIL WHEN YOU PREPARE YOURSELF AND LIVE WELL.

YOU CAN'T BLAME ME FOR YOUR BAGGAGE AND I PROMISE NOT TO BLAME YOU FOR MINE.

WHEN IT COMES TO THE PAST: WHAT'S DONE IS DONE-WHAT'S GONE IS GONE-LEARN A LESSON AND MOVE THE HELL ON!

WHY GRIEVE FOR WHAT YOU CAN NO LONGER HOLD? INSTEAD, CHERISH IT FOR WHAT IT WAS AND REMEMBER ALL YOU STILL HAVE—IT'S TIME TO LET GO OF THE PAST.

HOW CAN YOU EVER GROW TOO OLD WHEN YOU'RE SO YOUNG AT HEART, MIND, AND SOUL?

HOW CAN YOU BE STUCK OR STALE WHEN YOU HAVE A FRESH START EVERY DAY AT 12?

WHAT'S IT MATTER IF TODAY YOU'RE POOR FINANCIALLY, WHEN, WITH YOUR AWARE, CONSCIOUS, INFLUENTIAL MIND, YOU'RE EXTREMELY WEALTHY AND ABLE TO RECEIVE CONFIDENTLY. SO— EXERCISE YOUR INNER GENIUS!

Empowering Reflection

HOW CAN YOU HOLD ON TO RESENTMENT WITH SUCH AN INNER VOICE CONFIDENTLY DEVELOPING?

HOW CAN YOU BE UNDESIRABLE WHEN YOU'RE KIND, DELIGHTFUL, AND BEAUTIFUL?!

HOW CAN YOU HAVE A POOR SELF-IMAGE WHEN YOU'RE A TRUE PIECE OF ART, NOT YET FINISHED?

YOU CAN'T BE LOST AT SEA WHEN YOU HAVE A CHARTERED ROUTE FROM A TO B.

YOU CAN'T BE ALONE IN A WORLD OF OVER 8 BILLION, JUST LIKE YOU AND ME.

HOW CAN YOU BE AN UNDERDOG WITH ALL THIS FACTUAL DIALOGUE?

HOW CAN YOU REMAIN SO INTENSELY FILLED WITH ANGER OR FRUSTRATION AFTER READING THIS—REALIZING ALL THAT YOU WANT AND ALL THAT YOU CAN BRING INTO EXISTENCE!

YOU CAN'T FAIL AT ANYTHING IF YOU'RE CONSTANTLY LEARNING FROM EVERYTHING—GROWING AND BECOMING MORE WISE AND CAPABLE WITH EVERY PASSING DAY.

IT'S NOT ALWAYS ABOUT LIVING LONGER, BUT RATHER-LIVING BETTER!

TREAT TODAY AS IF IT'S YOUR BEST-NOT YOUR LAST!

HOW CAN YOU PASS ANY DAY UP-WHEN THAT'S ONE LESS DAY BEFORE YOUR TIME'S TRULY UP? AND WHEN IT'S YOUR TIME TO GO, THERE WON'T BE DAMN THING YOU CAN DO ABOUT IT. SO, UNTIL THEN, THINK POSITIVE, HAVE FAITH, AND KEEP FIGHTING—'TIL YOUR VERY LAST BREATH!

PRACTICE FOR TOMORROW-DON'T WAIT FOR OR TRY AND PREDICT IT.

REPEAT AFTER ME: "I GOT THIS—FOR ME!"

Empowering Reflection

Book Conclusion

There should be no controversy when using sound reason to positively influence others—helping support their intent for building a better life. Yet, there'll always be naysayers. This book, and I, personally, will likely be scrutinized and picked apart. *To those critics, I ask: What's your true motive? It certainly isn't to serve you or your audience in a positive way.*

This book is meant to enlighten, help heal, build up, inspire, and motivate.

Take the knowledge herein and apply it, just as you see fit. Your story is still unfolding, and I hope your journey is far, far from over. Some principles may not seem relevant today but they'll likely be in the future. That alone makes them worthy of your awareness. *Also, use this book as a guide for constructive conversation with others, such as with youth.*

The past only matters if it serves you—if it brings you joy or provides a lesson. Otherwise, yesterday is gone. Don't waste another day reliving what no longer benefits you. The present moment is all that's certain and it's what you should focus on. Make the most of the present, because this life, as you know it, will never happen again—not for you, not for me, not for anyone.

So, what do you want out of life? Do you want to start a business, find your soulmate, reshape your body, live pain-free, or do you dream of something a bit bigger, like helping to change the world for the better? Either way, the formula's the same: Dream, Practice, Believe, and Persist! Achieve, then move on to the next goal, all of which leading to your Ultimate Dream! Whether you're a doctor, teacher, mechanic, lawyer, cashier, farmer, or stay-at-home parent—*your mindset and lifestyle determine your success!*

You're free to seek additional research, case studies, and scientific backing for the principles, herein. However, know this: knowledge alone doesn't change lives—application does. If you commit to practicing the principles shared here, you'll experience their benefits just as profoundly as someone who's spent years studying these concepts—just like I have. Further research can prove of value, but only where curiosity and passion exist. Otherwise, take what you've reviewed, apply it, and let your own experience be your living proof. Then, share it with everyone you know! *Give to receive, remember?!*

Suggested Review Schedule:

- **Principle Section:** Revisit a time or two a year.
- **Wisdom Review:** Check in every month or so.
- **Practice Section:** Daily or weekly at first, then adjust as needed.

Just like a well-built structure needs regular maintenance, your well-being depends on your daily habits, stress level, and emotional balance. *Remember: A design is only as good as its upkeep!*

Use these principles to complement, not contradict, your core beliefs, such as religious values. However, if any of your long-held beliefs limit your happiness and personal growth, perhaps it's time to reevaluate them also.

Be aware of your Emissions and check your Baggage. Course-correct your thinking toward a more positive mindset. Listen to your heart and exercise your Inner Genius. Live a Lifestyle that persists and doesn't contradict, to produce a desirable return on investment. It sounds like a lot, but it's really not at all—this is how you'll achieve all you'll ever need and all you'll ever want!

Growth and wisdom are lifelong journeys. Don't limit yourself when seeking answers. Keep an open mind, explore what aligns with your intent, and make conscious choices that serve you best—and remember: ***a life ring alone will not save you—you still have to hold on and paddle!***

That being said, I've truly enjoyed my time with you and you should know, that my personal existence is not always positive–and I'm damn sure not perfect–*but I'm always accountable for my influence and my role in things.* This approach leaves me with no regrets–'cause it's all on me!

I truly hope you make the very most of your life–just as you dream, just as you practice for, and just as you feel's worthy of your time and all your positive effort!

'Til we meet again, take care!

Life's a collection of countless memories. So I hope you're makin' some damn good ones!

MJSmith

ENDNOTES

The concepts related to the *Mind & Body Connection* theory presented in this book are inspired in large part by the research and writings of Dr. M. T. Morter, Jr. and Dr. John E. Sarno.

Mentions of the *Law of Attraction* theory in this book are inspired by the work of Rhonda Byrne and her interpretation of the concept in *The Secret*.

My approach to *Personal Accountability* is greatly influenced by the teachings of John G. Miller.

LIVE TODAY AS IF IT'S YOUR BEST, NOT YOUR LAST

DON'T REGRET FOR SH%T. DON'T FEAR FOR SH%T EITHER

BE
A
MAGNET
FOR
GREATNESS!

GREATNESS

Life's
Loophole:
Awareness

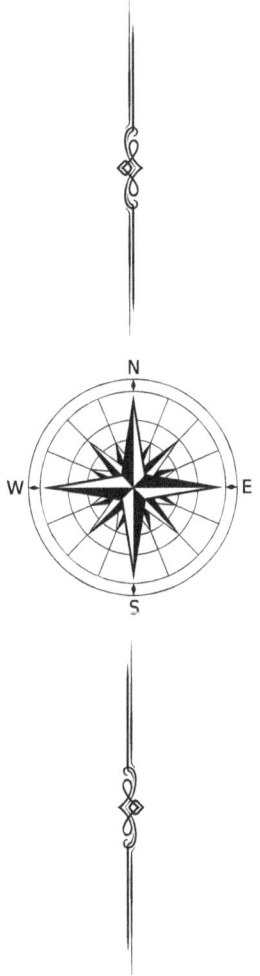

Awareness
For The
Human Mind
Used Not Only
For Surviving
But Also For
Thriving